ROD WAVE:

(Americans Singer)
HIS NEWEST ALBUM. "BEAUTIFUL MIND".

Oscar D. Noland.

TABLE OF CONTENT

CHAPTER 1:
WHO IS ROD WAVE?

Rapper Rod Wave, whose full name is Rodarius **Marcell Green**, is an up-and-coming recording artist from Florida. He is 22 years old and was born on August 27, 1999. Wave, a pioneer in the soul-trap genre, adds an aggressive mood to every song with his strong vocals.

Rod Wave started making music in 2015 and has since reaped the benefits of the social media age. With the publication of Heartbreak Hotel in 2016, he garnered popularity on SoundCloud. After that, he released a mixtape titled Hunger Games Vol.1 and then joined **Alamo Records.** Rod Wave's ability to seamlessly combine hip-hop and R&B has helped him continue to attract followers.

2019 saw Wave experience a truly meteoric rise to stardom as his song Heart on Ice became a hit on TikTok and YouTube. The song debuted at position 25 on the Billboard Hot 100. In the same year, Rod Wave also made his recording debut with Ghetto Gospel. Rags2Riches and SoulFly are the next two albums by Rod Wave, which were released in 2020 and 2021 respectively.

Additionally, he was included in XXL's 2020 Freshman Class. His position in the scene was so cemented. Wave's words and music are nonetheless impassioned despite his aggressiveness. This reminds him of a lot of the musicians he listened to growing up, including Kevin Gates and Kanye West.

His first studio album, "***Rookie of the Year***," was released in the year 2017. His most well-known songs are, to mention a few, "Tomorrow," "Heartbreak Hotel," and "Bag."

His most recent CD, Pray 4 Love, was launched and made available for purchase as the whole globe was coping with the Covid 19 issue.

His songs typically center on his family. His father was convicted of robbery and given a 6-year jail term while he was just in elementary school. However, according to media sources, he has a girlfriend by the name of Kelsey H from whom he also has two daughters.

With the release of his mixtape Hunger Games Vol.1, Rod's career got underway in 2016. Before joining Alamo Records, he independently released several mixtapes. He released his mixtape PTSD on June 14, 2019, and it included the song "Heart on Ice." The song gained enormous popularity on TikTok and YouTube and peaked at number 25 on the Billboard Hot 100. On November 1, 2019, Rod released his first album, Ghetto Gospel, which reached at number 10 on the US Billboard 200.

On April 3, 2020, Rod released his second album, Pray 4 Love. It debuted at number two on the Billboard 200, and a deluxe version was published on August 7. The song "Rags2Riches," which reached at number 12 on the Hot 100 and became his highest-charting single, was one of several from the album to make it into the Billboard Hot 100 chart.

Rod Wave joined the XXL 2020 Freshman Class on August 11, 2020. Rod Wave said he was working on his third album in an interview in July 2020; the album was supposed to be released on August 27, 2020.

He unveiled the tracklist for the album, Soulfly, on March 6, 2021. When Soulfly was released, it was YouTube's most-streamed album. It was published on March 26 and features Polo G just once, on the song "Richer."

His "candor and sly ability to pull at listeners' emotions" have earned him praise. "Music is a direct depiction of Rod's life, which is why he's cautious but open to collaborating with other musicians who share his enthusiasm," ABC News Radio's Rachel George said.

Green was reared in St. Petersburg, Florida, where he was born on August 27, 1999. His mother and father, who reared him, finally got divorced when he was in primary school. The fifth grade was when he started singing. Green graduated in 2017 from Lakewood High School, where he was a student.

Pray 4 Love, Green's second album, debuted at number two on the Billboard 200 upon release on April 3, 2020. A deluxe version followed on August 7. The song "Rags2Riches," which reached at number 12 on the Hot 100 and became his best charting single, was one of several on the album to make it into the Billboard Hot 100. Rod Wave was a member of XXL's 2020 Freshman Class as of August 11, 2020. His third album, which has not yet been given a title, was initially scheduled to be released on August 27, 2020.

Green was engaged in an almost catastrophic vehicle accident in the start of 2020. In the song "Through the Wire," which was released in July 2020, he discussed this.

ROD Wave is well renowned for being a soul-trap pioneer who also raps in hip-hop and R&B.

The song immediately became popular on TikTok and YouTube, reaching its highest point on the Billboard Hot 100 at number 25.

With his track Heart on Ice 1, Rod Wave debuted in 2019.
2019 saw the debut of Rod Wave, who debuted with the song Heart on Ice. Getty

He released his album Ghetto Gospel the same year, and it debuted at number 10 on the Billboard 200.

His two albums that came after, Pray 4 Love and SoulFly, both cracked the top 10. His fourth album, Beautiful Mind, which was postponed, is scheduled to be released on June 3, 2022.

But the record never materialized, leaving many fans dissatisfied.

Since his commercial success, Billboard has praised the musician for his "candor and deft ability to touch the hearts of fans."

How much money does Rod Wave have? Rod has received praise for his songs from all corners of the business, and he has been nominated for the best new artist at the Billboard Music Awards in 2021.

He has 5.1 million Instagram followers as of June 2022.

According to the successbug, he has a $3 million net worth.

According to reports, Rod and his unknown companion are the parents of twin children.

In 2021, the couple welcomed their twins.

The rapper has so far decided to keep his girlfriend and girls anonymous and out of the spotlight.

But when he spoke openly about the difficulties of being a young parent on

The Breakfast Club in April 2022, he brought them up.

I'm so accustomed to being able to just get on a plane and travel anyplace, but that s**t made me want to stay here instead of going anywhere else, he added.

Wave was detained on a criminal accusation of violence by strangulation, it was announced on May 2, 2022.

He was charged with choking his ex-girlfriend inside their house while their two kids were there, according to an arrest warrant affidavit at the time.

On May 19, 2022, the Osceola County Attorney's Office said they will no longer be pursuing charges in the case.

Bradford Cohen, Rod Wave's attorney, told Rolling Stone that the incident was the result of a miscommunication between a girlfriend and a lover.

"Mr. Green was arrested as a consequence of the misunderstanding."

CHAPTER 2:
HIS NEWEST ALBUM

These days, Rod Wave is undeniably a fan favorite, and for good reason. Although he has only been active for five years, the St. Petersburg, Florida, the musician has been smoothly coasting to the top with each release despite his short tenure in the industry.

Rod Wave is already in his own lane and performing in the studio the way that suits him best since almost all of his albums have achieved platinum status so far. The 22-year-old is without a doubt one of the few artists in today's younger age that stands out from his work ethic alone, and it is something that will never go unnoticed.

Rod Wave releases his fourth studio album, Beautiful Mind, to the public today (Aug. 12).

Rod Wave broke some news around two months ago that swiftly reached followers all across the globe. On June 13, he tweeted, "On my baby's dis my last sad ass album I'm off dat jus want to live happy travel grab dis money," indicating that he is done with the dismal songs.

Wave is primarily recognized for his "Debbie Downer" music, which not many people like, but it is encouraging to see that he is shifting gears and pushing ahead this time. The album Beautiful Mind is Wave's follow-up to 2021's Soulfly (which is RIAA certified platinum as of July 26, 2022).

Rod Wave, who has 24 tracks in all, only taps on Jack Harlow and December Joy, keeping his features to a bare minimum. It is wonderful to watch Beautiful Mind come to life after experiencing some setbacks lately! View it right now.

With his own style of pain music—a melodic rap with R&B influences that exposes the misery of the hustle—Rod Wave has shot to stardom. Nobody is more aware of how unexpected his rise from the Florida streets to sold-out concerts with rapt crowds is than Wave, who expresses this sentiment in his new song "Stone Rolling."

Wave composes over a depressing tempo fueled by a mellow guitar tune from a location where his trip aspirations have come true. He sings yearningly of a future with roots—one without drugs, without leeches in his circle, and with a place on the beach for his children—for a fleeting moment when the grip that his fast-paced existence throws over him breaks. The adage "the grass is always greener" and the idea that there is some truth to cliches are both clichés. However, Rod Wave's voice has a way of making even the most worn-out clichés seem fresh.

"Rolling stone" lyrics below.

Pipe that shit up TNT

SephGotTheWaves

He's a rolling stone, he's a rolling stone

Long as the wind blows, I'll be long gone

He's a rolling stone, he's a rolling stone

Driving many miles and roads, and still can't find

My, my home

I remember being a kid, I just wanted to travel

On my bed, writing raps thinkin' 'bout daddy

Was in my cell writing raps, regretting my actions

Like if I make it out this shit, I'm going straight to Cali

It's like, I know my mama love him, but I still hate him

*Living life like a runaway and it's
six years later*

I said it and no, I don't regret it

*I just woke up on my tour bus, I
don't know where I'm headed*

*I been out here on my own since I
turned eighteen*

*Packed my bags, hit the road, left
to chase my dreams*

*Loved livin' in the A when people
knew me, barely*

*Then my dream came alive, that
shit got very scary*

*I got so much in love for Houston
like it raised me*

Me and Sauce in a Maybach, getting faded

This don't feel right, nah, this shit feel crazy

Cluthin' on my pipe, don't even feel like I made it

I love Las Vegas, but that was before I was famous

Look, I traveled across the nation, don't matter what state we in

People stop and stare, and looking at us like aliens

I spent some time in Carolina, spent time in Tennessee

Is there a heaven for a G? Where can I go to get some peace?

I wanna settle with my kids, buy a crib by the beach

No more 'Perc's to ease the pain and no more drank to go to sleep

He's a rolling stone, he's a rolling stone

Long as the wind blows, I'll be long gone

He's a rolling stone, he's a rolling stone

Driving many miles and roads, and still can't find

My, my home

Yeah, Yeah

My, my home

Life of a rolling stone, life of a rolling stone..

Currently, rod wave is signed to two different record labels, interscope records and Geffen records.

His social media handles:
Instagram @rodwave
Twitter @ rodwave.

www.ingramcontent.com/pod-product-compliance
Lightning Source LLC
Chambersburg PA
CBHW070826170726
48000CB00019B/2754